Revolutionary Credit Repair Secrets

Cardinal Rules to Eliminate Negative Items From Your Credit Report and Get a Perfect Score

Copyright 2016- Michael McCord- All rights reserved.

This document is geared towards providing exact and reliable information in regards to the topic and issue covered. The publication is sold with the idea that the publisher is not required to render accounting, officially permitted, or otherwise, qualified services. If advice is necessary, legal or professional, a practiced individual in the profession should be ordered.

- From a Declaration of Principles which was accepted and approved equally by a Committee of the American Bar Association and a Committee of Publishers and Associations.

In no way is it legal to reproduce, duplicate, or transmit any part of this document in either electronic means or in printed format. Recording of this publication is strictly prohibited and any storage of this document is not allowed unless with written permission from the publisher. All rights reserved.

The information provided herein is stated to be truthful and consistent, in that any liability, in terms of inattention or otherwise, by any usage or abuse of any policies, processes, or directions contained within is the solitary and utter responsibility of the recipient reader. Under no circumstances will any legal responsibility or blame be held against the publisher for any reparation, damages, or monetary loss due to the information herein, either directly or indirectly.

Respective authors own all copyrights not held by the publisher.

Table Of Contents

Introduction 4

Chapter 1: Your FICO Score 6

Chapter 2: Your Credit Reports 17

Chapter 3: Creating a Credit Repair Plan 26

Chapter 4: Improving Your Past 33

Chapter 5: Keep Boosting Your Credit 38

Chapter 6: Common Mistakes 41

Conclusion 47

Introduction

Cancer, job loss, divorce, injury, sometimes life just hammers us. What you thought had been manageable debts suddenly become overwhelming. Or, maybe you just had a rough patch and missed or were late on a couple of payments. Suddenly, your "good" credit score becomes "poor," or even worse, you had to file for bankruptcy and your credit was ruined.

How do you recover from a bad credit rating?

It may seem like trying to rebuild your credit score is an impossible task. You may even wonder why you should try, particularly after bankruptcy since your credit score is going to be pretty bad for a long time (which isn't necessarily true).

It is worth it. A great credit score saves you money, makes it easier for you to get credit (even if you've filed for Chapter 7 bankruptcy), and improves your job prospects.

Believe it or not, prospective employers often reject candidates for openings just because of their credit score. While it may not be fair, an employer can suspect that an employee in financial trouble will be more likely to misappropriate business assets. A poor credit score will usually result in higher car insurance bills too, so there's another reason for improving your credit score.

You may find this surprising, but even right after a bankruptcy filing, you will have companies contacting you offering credit cards, car loans, and other ways to borrow money. While many of these offers will be for "secured" credit cards (you put up the money for the card's debt limit as security), some of them will be for unsecured credit cards (they'll have a very low balance, but they'll still be a credit card). It's not as crazy as it sounds. After a bankruptcy filing your debt to income ratio should be much improved, and since you can't file again for bankruptcy for from seven to 10 years, become a more attractive candidate to them (particularly if you kept your house after bankruptcy and you have some equity in it). Of course, they will expect you to pay higher interest rates on your credit usage, and often want you to start with a secured credit card where you fund the card and they loan you your own money.

As you improve your credit score, credit becomes cheaper, and easier to get, in turn making it easier and easier to prove your credit worthiness (and also to get into debt trouble again too). Earn a perfect credit score, and you become a rock star. Lenders will fall all over themselves offering you loans and credit cards, and at the best rates!

In this e-book you'll get the information you need to boost your credit score and reach that highly coveted perfect score. It provides a wealth of information, and also includes useful phone numbers, mailing addresses, and web pages to help you. All of these have been checked and verified as of September 2016 to make sure they're up to date.

Chapter 1:
Your FICO Score

Let's get started.

As you know, credit is all about numbers. Numbers for the amount of money owed, numbers for the credit available, number of years your credit accounts have existed and other numbers. Of course one of the most important numbers is for your credit score.

It's an interesting concept. You have a single number that represents your credit worthiness. You can walk into any car dealer or bank and can proudly announce, "I've got a ... credit score" and know they will want to lend you their money or sell you their cars, and at a great interest rate to boot!

There's only one problem with that concept. You're probably not using the same credit score number your lender is. The dirty little secret is that the credit score number you hear about all the time, the same one you might have even paid money to get, isn't really the one lenders use to figure out your credit risk and what interest rate they offer you. You see, there isn't one number that everybody gets. The industry standard is the "FICO" number; the original credit score number created almost three decades ago by Fair, Isaac and Company (now FICO), a San Jose, CA based data analytics company.

While this is the "number" everyone thinks of when they talk about credit scores, there isn't even one FICO score number since the company keeps updating its way of compiling it. The FICO Score 8 model is what's been in use, but the firm has already released the FICO Score 9 model which many lenders are now using.

But wait. There's more! The company also offers the FICO Auto Score (models 2, 3, 4, 5, and 8 are currently in use) and the FICO Bankcard Score (models 2, 3, 4, 5, and 8). Of course FICO has also just released the 9th model of these scores as well.

In fairness to the company, things do change over time. The idea behind the score is to provide a creditor with a predictive tool as to whether a consumer is a good risk for a loan or not. During the past 25 years the score has been in existence there have been enough changes to make newer and newer models necessary. FICO also maintains that industry specific models are necessary to meet the special needs of those industries.

It may be reasonable, it may just be a sales pitch to banks and auto dealers, but either way, it means they're using a different FICO number than you are (if you've even gotten your true FICO score). And, while the general FICO score range runs from 350-800, the Auto and Bankcard scores range from 200-900. Your "FICO" scores for these models will probably be lower than the FICO score you think you have too.

A lot of things good and bad can affect your credit score. FICO, the company that provides your FICO credit score (which the company says is used by 95% of the United States' largest financial institutions), bases your score on five factors. According to the www.myfico.com web site, it breaks those factors down like this:

- Payment history: this history accounts for 35% of your credit score

- Amounts owed: your current debt load accounts for 30% of your credit score

- Length of your credit history: how long you've had credit accounts for 15% of your credit score

- Credit mix: most people have a mix of debts from credit cards, loans, and other bills. Your mix of these debts accounts for 10% of your FICO number

- New credit: taking on new credit via credit cards or loans accounts for 10% of your credit score (and the inquiries these lenders initiate also affects your score)

As you can see, there are a lot of different considerations that go into producing a credit score. The breakdown above also gives you several different ways to influence that score as well.

This is important information. It's what you're going to use to build your credit repair plan. Let's face it. When you have five different areas to work on, and seven years or more worth of history to account for, "winging it" is hardly a sound approach. You need to consider what you can do quickly and easily and what is going to take more time and effort.

Before you get to that point though, you should start by doing your homework. Fortunately, your first step in the research project that is your financial life history is pretty easy and absolutely free. Request your most recent credit reports.

Also, while trying to improve your FICO credit score is a good thing, you're also trying to improve your credit report in general. Still, doing things to improve your credit score will generally strengthen your credit report too.

Oh, one other thing. While your Fico credit score may range from 300 to 850, creditors aren't necessarily using the same score you are. Sometimes they rely on scores provided by the credit reporting companies, which are not FICO scores even though they may seem like they are (they are calculated the same way though).

FICO also has several different ratings products. Beside FICO, you may have also heard of the Vantage score. This is similar to the FICO score and in fact, uses the same 300 to 850 scale in its latest version. Finally, check the fine print of any web site offering your credit score. You'll find just about all of them are giving you a credit score and not a true FICO score. If nothing else though, these numbers are useful for tracking your credit improvement efforts. They're usually calculated on the same information as your FICO score and using the same formula.

FICO Score Breakdowns

While your FICO score is an individual number, creditors use it in comparison to other customers. They break these down into ranges of scores and then rate them as to risk. Improving your credit score from one range to the next may only take a few points and can qualify you for lower interest rates, increased credit limits, and make you eligible for new offers.

According to FICO, there are eight ranges in its FICO Score 8 data (one of several of the company's products). These ranges are:

- 300-499: 4.9% of the population fall into this category
- 500-549: 7.6% fall into this range
- 550-599: 9.4% fall into this range
- 600-649: 10.3% fall into this range

If your credit rating is between 300 and 629, you are considered a bad credit risk. If it is between 630 and 689, you are considered a fair credit risk. These numbers may seem arbitrary, but if you consider the percentage of consumers for each of the ranges, it makes some sense. Let's continue looking at FICO score ranges:

- 650-699: 13% of the population fall into this range

- 700-749: 16% fall into this range

- 750-799: 18.2% fall into this range

- 800-850: 19.9% fall into this range

If your credit score is between 690 and 719, you are considered a good credit risk. If it is between 720 and 850, you are considered an excellent credit risk. If your credit score is above 700, you're in the top 54% of all consumers. This may not be quite what you expected to hear. A 700 out of 850 sounds pretty good doesn't it? But being in the top 54% doesn't put you in position for the best rates. All it means is that your credit rating is about average.

While your main goal is to get your credit score as close to 850 as possible, moving up a range or ranges will still benefit you in the short term. For one thing, the closer you get to 850, the slower your advance will be, and the more you'll suffer for any credit transgressions.

As you improve your credit score, you should know the higher the credit score, the more severe the penalties charged to your score are. If you have a credit score of 680 and your property is foreclosed, you'll lose from 85 to 105 points. If you have a credit score of 780 and your property is foreclosed, you'll lose from 140 to 160 points. You don't want to make credit mistakes at any time, but obviously it's even more important if you have a high credit score and want to maintain that score.

Getting Your Credit Score

Some credit cards, such as the Discover Card, will provide your credit score when you log into your online account. If you don't have access via this method, don't worry. There are several sites that will give you the information in return for you allowing ads on their web sites. Don't worry about these sites triggering inquiry counts. Inquiries from you, the consumer, don't count against your credit score or credit report.

These sites don't ask for a credit card to "verify" your information. This is always a good sign. They shouldn't ask for your full social security number either since the other information they request plus the last four digits of your SSN should be enough. Keep in mind, sites such as these need to pay the bills somehow. For the ones listed here, the usual approach is either on page advertisements or "advice" on credit vehicles that can help your credit score. They also tend to offer upgraded account options that provide additional information or more frequent credit score updates. Identify theft protection is another product these sites usually offer. You don't have to buy anything to get your credit score number and other useful information from them though. Just remember, these are usually not true "FICO" numbers even though they are calculated on the same information and use the same formula (as at least one of the FICO models).

Credit Sesame

This is a free web site (www.creditsesame.com). Once you create an account and provide the information it needs to verify your identity, it provides your credit score and a brief insight into your credit situation for five categories (payment history, credit usage, credit age, account mix, and inquiries for the past 12 months). The rest of your page provides links for credit card offers the site says can help improve your credit as well as some brief financial advice such as how much money should be in your emergency savings account (recommending a bank in the process) Credit Sesame uses TransUnion for its information. It does not ask for a credit card to "verify" your information or gain access to the site. The site will also email you an updated credit score the first of each month.

Credit Karma

Credit Karma (www.creditkarma.com) provides both your TransUnion and Equifax credit score numbers. It also provides various offers that may help you improve your credit. This site also doesn't ask for a credit card number. This site also provides additional helpful information about your credit history, including giving you access to information in your TransUnion and Equifax credit reports.

This is another site that provides helpful information to the consumer trying to manage their credit wisely.

Quizzle

Quizzle (www.quizzle.com) also provides you with access to your TransUnion and Equifax credit scores. No credit card information is necessary to get this information. Like the others, you'll receive offers for various credit products. A nice feature of this service is a credit score analysis, which not only shows what's wrong with your credit history, but also offers advice as to how you can improve your credit score. A nice extra is that this site also provides your Vantage credit score (This is another credit score creditors use. Its most recent version, VantageScore 3, uses the same 300 to 850 scale that FICO does.) Unlike the FICO score, which is calculated individually for each of the three credit reporting firms, the VantageScore 3 incorporates information from all three credit reporting firms and the calculates a score from that information.

There are some pretty useful tools on this site in addition to the credit score analysis. For instance, it provides a timeline of your credit history, has a trending page that displays your credit score, credit utilization, available credit, and account balance trends. One other thing, when I signed up for a Quizzle account, my confirmation email took a bit longer than any of the other sites. It wasn't any big deal, just 10 or 15 minutes, but when you're used to instant responses you end up wondering if your request didn't go through. Just be patient. The site is useful enough to worth waiting a few minutes.

Lending Tree

Lending Tree (www.lendingtree.com), is another free site where you can get your credit score. Like the others, the site provides offers for credit cards that will help you improve your score. Unlike the other sites you've learned about so far, Lending Tree is also a lender offering mortgages, auto and personal loans. It also provides some useful information about your credit history.

Credit.com

Credit.com (www.credit.com) is worth considering because it's the only one of the free credit score web sites to provide you with your Experion credit score. Like the others, no credit card is required to sign up. This site isn't quite as easy to read or as navigable as the others discussed so far, but it is still very useable. Like the others, it provides your rating (from A+ to F) for each of the five FICO score categories. Many of its links that look like they would lead to someplace helpful instead tend to lead you to ads for credit repair services.

The site does offer an "Action Plan" for you, but it's basic ("Pay your bills," "Keep your debt low," "Repair your credit").

Discover

Discover is now offering a free look at your FICO score at its www.discover.com. According to the web site, it is using your information from Experion. The web page also shows you what's helping your credit score and what's hurting it and provides tabs that provide detail on your FICO score categories. It does promote the company's credit card products, but it does so sparingly.

A really helpful feature of the Discover site is that you can download and save your credit scorecard. The scorecard updates once a month, so you can download a new one each month. Save them to your credit score improvement file so you can keep track of your progress and look for things you can improve.

In the Frequently Asked Questions section of the web page Discover says the number you're given is the actual FICO Score 8 number based on the Experian credit report. It also points out that different credit reports can provide different information and different score models will also produce different results. Since the Discover.com credit scorecard is free, provides useful information, and has pretty good information, it's definitely worth using. It also shows how confusing getting a handle on your credit can be.

So Why All the Different Numbers?

It seems pretty confusing doesn't it? There are different scoring models, different companies offering their own scoring models, and, there are the credit reporting agencies as well.

In theory, the three companies should be listing and comparing the same information on you. The reality is they often have some discrepancies (another reason for checking all three), plus there is at least a little subjectivity in the credit evaluation process.

The lesson from this I guess is life is confusing. While it would be nice to have just one number to worry about, for various reasons, that's just not going to happen.

How Long Will it Take?

This depends on your situation. Some things don't stay on a credit report that long; others stay a long time. There are certainly ways of improving your credit score in a relatively short period of time, and almost anyone can achieve some kind of improvement, but there are some things that take a while. For instance, building your credit score after a bankruptcy is very possible and you can make progress quickly, but getting to a perfect credit score isn't going to happen very quickly. It takes seven (Chapter 13) to 10 (Chapter

7) years for a bankruptcy to clear from your credit report. It may be possible to get one off your report sooner, but you can still raise your credit score significantly.

If you are trying to rebuild your credit after a bankruptcy, you can boost your credit rating fairly quickly. It's easier to raise your score when it's low, than it is when it's high.

Chapter 2:
Your Credit Reports

As you probably know, there are three nationwide credit reporting companies: Experian, TransUnion, and Equifax. Thanks to a law passed by the federal government a few years ago, you are entitled to one free credit report from each of these companies every 12 months. You can do this by contacting each company individually, or by taking advantage of the FTC (Federal Trade Commission) authorized web site. If you're not comfortable using this approach, there is also a phone number you can use to request these reports. Here are both options:

www.annualcreditreport.com

1-877-322-8228

Be careful when going to a credit report web site. As the FTC web site points out, there have web sites that claim to offer "free credit reports," that actually only offer a free trial followed by a monthly fee automatically charged to your credit card. Use the authorized web site only.

The process for requesting your free credit reports is pretty easy, and the web site tries to make the process as simple as possible:

Fill out a form online at the authorized web site.

Chose the reports you want to request (you can ask for one from each reporting company or pick and chose the report or reports you want to see). If you already have a good handle on your credit, then you can plan on staggering your requests asking for one every four months so you can better track your credit.

Provide verification that you are actually asking for your reports and not someone else's. This verification process will ask you about items from your credit history. It WILL NOT ask you for a credit card to verify your identity. If you are at a web site that does, you are not at the authorized web site even if it says your card will not be charged.

Print out or download your reports from each company you've requested the information from. You can save your reports as .pdf files, which can be stored on your computer or printed out. Since these reports can be pretty long (40, 50 pages or more), you might think twice about printing them out in their entirety.

Be aware, these reports will not include your credit score. You'll have to take a different route to get that as noted in the previous chapter. Ironically, you don't really need to know your credit score to improve it, and your credit reports are what you need to start. Before you learn about that, remember, no part of the credit report request process requires payment or a credit card. This e-book has provided you with some web sites where you can learn your credit score for free, so you will have access to that information.

Once you've downloaded your credit reports, it's time to go over them to understand your position and identify what's hurting your credit rating. You can then start identifying what you need to do to improve your situation. Let's look at each section and see what you can do. Keep in mind, each credit reporting company organizes the information it provides differently, so you may need to set up your own ledger to organize the data. Also pay close attention to anything that doesn't make sense or you don't remember. If you see the name of a lender you don't recognize there's a chance it doesn't belong in your account and got their by accident.

Since you're trying to improve your credit score, one sensible approach would be to create a log or spread sheet for each of FICO's five areas. Of course, even with this approach, make sure you check the personal information each report contains. Make sure each report identifies you correctly by name and personal information. If there's a name that doesn't match yours, or an address that is wrong, it could be a warning indication that there's someone else's information in your report. Your goal should be to fix every mistake you find, because even small things might affect your credit score.

Here's how to use this approach:

Credit History

Equifax, like TransUnion and Experian, provides your credit history (or summary or something else that means the same thing) early in its credit report. Review each account it displays, looking for ones that don't belong in the report, or errors in the account information.

The Equifax report includes a color coded payment history for each account (although that history may be reported as not available) that shows when payments were made on time, late by 30 days, late by 60 days, and beyond all the way out to 180 days late. Also look at how many inquiries you've had the past two years, since inquiries also affect your credit score. Keep in mind that only a few types of inquiries stay on your report for two years. The others (including many of the ones you're concerned about) stay on your record for only a year.

TransUnion on the other hand begins with personal information followed by adverse accounts (if you have any), followed by satisfactory accounts. It also provides a color coded payment history and record of late payments.

Experion also gets to your account history early, but begins with your personal information first, followed by potentially negative items, then your account history. (By the way, it's a good idea to check your personal information for mistakes too, particularly if the wrong version of your name is included. It's always possible that someone else's name has been included in your report by mistake.) While it also documents your payment history and late payments, it skips the color coding the other two companies use.

Things to look for when reviewing your credit history:

Payment history: unsurprisingly, creditors think paying bills on time is a big part of credit worthiness. Late payments can hurt your score. Defaults are even worse.

Inquiries: the more you have that have to do with getting and using credit, the greater the affect it can have on your credit scores. Look at the ones you have and their initiation dates. Try to reduce the number of these inquires down as much as possible. Simply doing nothing will help you make progress, provided you don't try to borrow money or open a new credit card or request a credit increase. "Testing the waters" to see what kind of car loan you can get is a good example of what not to do, unless you are actually planning on buying a car in the next few weeks. Inquiries you make about your own credit history do not affect your credit score.

Things that significantly hurt your credit score: bankruptcies, foreclosures, lawsuits, wage attachments, liens, and judgments. If there are any in your credit history that you think you can challenge and get them removed mark them. A bankruptcy for instance, costs your credit score anywhere from 130 to 240 points (the higher your credit score at the time of the bankruptcy, the bigger the point penalty).

Late payments: the FICO web site says it considers things like how late these payments were, how much was owed, how recent are they, and how many there are.

Amounts Owed

This is another category that significantly affects your credit score and credit worthiness. Owing a lot isn't automatically a negative though. If you have a good track record of paying bills before they're due and aren't near your credit limit, credit debt can actually help your credit score. There are several things FICO takes into consideration when trying to determine whether or not your debt load is an issue. These include:

- Total amount owed: this is the amount you owe on all your accounts including secured loans such as mortgages and car loans and unsecured loans such as credit cards and signature loans.

- Debt distribution: how is your debt distributed amongst your accounts?

- Debt to credit ratio on revolving accounts: using your credit doesn't necessarily hurt your credit worthiness; in fact it can help it. If you get to the point though where your debit is close to your credit limit then your credit score will suffer. Zero debt isn't a guarantee of the best credit score either. Often a low debt to credit ratio gets the best results.

- Current balances: FICO warns that the current balances amounts it uses are those provided from your creditors, so your view of your balance may not match the one FICO uses in calculating your credit score.

- How many accounts have balances: the greater the number of your accounts that are carrying the balances, the greater the chance of your credit being over extended is according to FICO.

- Amount you owe on installment debt: this is things like car loans, personal loans and other situations where you've borrowed a specific amount and agreed to pay back a certain amount each month until the loan has been paid off. The higher the percentage of these debts you've paid off, the more it helps your FICO score.

You can probably get some idea of things you can do to improve your credit score when looking at these criteria. If not, you'll learn about them in the upcoming chapters.

As you review your credit report, look for things that you've had particular trouble with in the past. Consider grouping report problems either from easiest to hardest to solve, or by FICO score category. Also, make sure your credit limits are accurate. If you've gotten an increase in your limit, and it hasn't shown up on your credit report, that may be costing your credit score some points. Figure that anything occurred more than 45 days in the past should definitely been on your credit report.

Length of Credit History

Obviously, a combination of long credit history and reliable payments is ideal for a strong credit rating. A short credit history can still boost your score though provided you don't have any late or missed payments.

There are other factors as well. How long have your accounts been active? A long credit history with lots of account closings and openings can be a bad sign. How long it's been since you've used an account can also affect your credit score. The longer it's been since the account has been used, the more likely it is to be closed by the issuer too. An account closure changes your available credit total, removes an older account (usually) and changes your debt to credit ratio; three things that affect your score in a negative way.

Credit Mix

How you use your credit tools also plays a role in how you're viewed by creditors. It's not a big role, but in the absence of other indicators, it can become a factor. According to www.myfico.com, someone with a history of credit cards and payments will score better than someone who's never used credit cards. Don't open accounts just to have more accounts, the site cautions. That doesn't look good either. Also, opening a new account also generates another credit inquiry, which can also ding your credit score. Closed accounts remain on your credit report (for seven years), as does the information they contain.

New Credit

Don't plan on opening a bunch of new credit accounts thinking it will help boost your credit score Fico says. It's often a warning that someone is over extended and is turning to credit to make ends meet.

Another way opening new accounts affects your credit score is by lowering the average account age number, something that also dings your credit scores. It also generates inquiries, which also lower your credit score.

As you read earlier, credit inquiries can affect your credit score, but how much they cost you and whether they cost you or not are a bit more complicated than you might have expected.

First off, FICO categorizes credit inquires as "hard" and "soft" inquiries. Soft inquiries (such as your reviewing your credit report) don't affect your credit scores. Hard inquiries (such as those requested by loan and credit card issuers in response to your request for credit) can dock your credit score about five points said the FICO web site. However, if you're rate shopping (something FICO says is a good thing) for say, a mortgage, all inquiries related to that credit account that occur within 45 days of the new credit account opening, will count as just one inquiry.

Your recent credit history can also be a big help in reducing the damage of late payments and missed payments in the past. "Late payments in the past can be overcome," the web site said, "re-establishing credit and making payments on time will raise a FICO score over time." Most credit card companies like to see a customer who has recovered from credit problems and is now using their credit wisely.

Tri-Merge Credit Report

If you've ever applied for a loan, you've probably heard your lender use the term "Tri-Merge Credit Report." This is simply a combination of all three credit reporting companies credit reports and credit scores. It may surprise you to know that the scores these credit reporting firms use are not true FICO scores, but just their own version of a credit score. In fact, the three companies don't even use the same numerical scale. Experion uses a 330-830 scale, TransUnion uses a 300-850 scale, and Equifax uses a 280-850 scale.

If you feel you need to see your Tri-merge credit report, you'll have to go to a credit monitoring agency (and likely pay a fee) to get a copy of it. You could get a Tri-merge from one of the big three credit reporting services, but you'll only get one credit score, hence the suggestion to use a credit monitoring agency, which provides all three.

You can find an example of a Tri-merge report here.

Chapter 3:
Creating a Credit Repair Plan

Now that you've reviewed your credit reports, credit scores, and credit history, you're ready to start thinking about what you can do to start pushing it upwards. Take each category of the FICO credit score, look at your history, and ask how you can improve that category.

If you've completed the process you learned in the previous chapter, you're now ready to start building your credit repair plan. You should begin by grouping problems you identified from your credit report review in a way that makes most sense to you.

Consider creating a separate email account for your credit rating efforts. This will make it easier to keep related emails organized.

Here's one approach to organizing your tasks:

Quick and easy: if you have some credit inquiries that will expire soon, there's nothing you really need to do, except be careful about applying for new credit. Using some of your savings to reduce your debt load on a credit card that's near its limit is pretty simple, so long as you have the money to do so.

Moderate effort: if you found any discrepancies in any of your credit reports, you should contact the appropriate credit reporting company to see if you can get the error corrected. Remember, both the credit reporting companies and creditors "... are responsible for correcting inaccurate or incomplete information in your credit report," according to the FTC. Each of the three companies concerned have web pages specifically for customer disputes. Here are the links:

- Experian phone number: 1-866-200-6020 (this is the number to request a credit report, Experian strongly prefers consumers use its online dispute page)

- Experian mailing address: Experian, P.O. Box 4500, Allen, TX 75013 (you can send a dispute to this address)

- Web address for filing a dispute: https://www.experian.com/help/

- Equifax phone number for filing a dispute: 866 349-5191

- Equifax mailing address: Equifax Information Services, LLC., P.O. Box 740256, Atlanta, GA 30348

- Web address for filing a dispute:

- https://experian.referral.equifax.com/CreditInvestigation/home.action

- TransUnion: phone number for filing a dispute, 800-916-8800

- Mailing address: TransUnion LLC Consumer Dispute Center P.O. Box 2000 Chester, PA 19016

- Web address for filing a dispute:

https://www.transunion.com/credit-disputes/dispute-your-credit

More effort: you can probably get a creditor to remove a late payment from your account record (more on this in a few lines). Another strategy you can consider is to take out a debt consolidation loan (more on this in a few lines too). It's a riskier strategy, so it needs to be carefully considered.

If you've found a discrepancy on your credit report, writing a letter to the responsible credit reporting company should be one of the first things you do. The FTC even provides you with a sample letter at its web site. Here's a link to it:

https://www.consumer.ftc.gov/articles/0384-sample-letter-disputing-errors-your-credit-report

The FTC recommends you send the letter via certified mail "return receipt requested." It also says to include copies (not originals) of any relevant documents or receipts you have. It can also help to send a copy of the page from your credit report with the item(s) circled. You can find more information at the FTC web page on this topic:

https://www.consumer.ftc.gov/articles/0058-credit-repair-how-help-yourself - diy

While you can probably get things done via company web sites, going the paper route gives you a physically documented record of your efforts. While you hopefully won't need it, hard evidence can be easier to work with and be stronger than electronic records.

Get Your Stuff Together

It helps to be organized. Create a binder or file and start gathering any records that will help you make your case with the various companies you're going to need to communicate with. Make sure you have either web sites or email addresses for your creditors. Small businesses might not offer much when it comes to web sites, but you can count on the major credit card companies to have functional web sites that include ways you can contact them for help or disputes. They usually have live help available online too. Remember, if you're communicating in real time be prepared ahead of time and have at least an outline of what you want to cover in your call. This is one advantage of using the mail to make your dispute, you're much more likely to submit all the necessary proof. Make sure you have the original of everything you sent in your dispute.

Your Checklist

Put together a checklist with deadlines to help keep you on track. Organize by approach you like best. You can go from easy to hard, get going on the stuff that will take longer to get a response on, then knock off the faster stuff, so while the slow moving chores and winding their way through the mail or a company bureaucracy, you can be getting things done.

Removing late payment codes: try to get as many of these removed as you can. Late payments take seven years to clear from your credit history, so trying to get as many as you can removed can be a big help.

Correcting errors: misspellings, incorrect information, and erroneous accounts. Credit bureaus have 30 days to investigate your complaint. You can use the mail system or web site for Equifax or TransUnion. Experian only accepts requests online. You can find phone numbers, web addresses, and mail addresses for each company (if offered) here. One thing to look at extra closely is anything listed by collections agencies. Consumer debt has a legal expiration date. Once that date has passed, you can't be forced to pay it. Collection agencies can still make an effort to collect that debt and will still sell the debt to other collectors who then try their luck collecting the debt. In the process, the dates recorded for that debt can be misreported requiring correction. Of course if a debt collector contacted you and you agreed to pay anything back (whether you paid any money or not) the clock on the debt begins from that point on.

Reducing debt ratios on credit cards: try to avoid having any cards that are near their limits if you can. Considering transferring a balance if you can do so without doing anything to make your report worse (such as applying for a new card to transfer the balance to). Paying down the cards is ideal if you have the money.

Disputing items: this is a little different than correcting errors. Here you're trying to get items off your report that maybe are justified. Still, if you can convince the creditor to remove the item, it's to your advantage, and let's face it, it's not like you're going to bully a big credit card company into doing something it doesn't want to do. Even disputing an old negative charge can sometimes pay off simply because the creditor may not respond.

Clearing civil judgments: these also appear on your credit history, so if you can pay them off or get them discharged it will benefit your credit score.

Should You Dispute with the Credit Report Company or the Creditor?

This is an important question. If you're trying to dispute an error on your credit report, you should definitely take that up with the credit reporting agencies since they are required to conduct an investigation under the Fair Credit Reporting Act, the regulation that also requires the credit reporting agencies to provide your free yearly credit reports. If you send the dispute to a creditor instead, that requirement isn't triggered, and you don't get the protections the act offers (such as the ability to sue the credit reporting agency in question).

Be Prepared

The credit reporting firms tell you using their online dispute web pages is fast and easily. Of course if you file your dispute too quickly and leave out some relevant information, it's your situation that suffers not theirs. If you're providing extra information in the appropriate blank on your credit report, you might find it doesn't offer enough room (hmm... strange how the small space limits the information you can provide). Since it is your situation that matters to you, take the harder and more time consuming route. Make sure you have all the documentation you need and provide a detailed letter explaining your dispute. If the online dispute page doesn't let you do this, then end your dispute in by certified mail, return receipt requested. These things may only be important in a worst case scenario where you need to go to court, but if things get to that worst case, you'll be glad you did. And even if the credit reporting company doesn't use all that information, you've still taken away the argument that you never provided enough information in your dispute. You can also sent a copy of the materials to the creditor who the dispute involves as well just so they can't argue they didn't have the necessary information either.

Chapter 4: Improving Your Past

Raising your credit score calls for a two pronged attack. The first part of it is doing everything you can to re-write the past. Every negative you can get removed will help to boost your score. This is why you're going over your credit report with a fine tooth comb. Correcting or getting rid of an existing notice can have a bigger impact than some of the actions you do in the future.

Taking Care of the Easy Stuff

The first steps in trying to improve your credit score revolve around things you can get done with as little time and effort as possible. One thing that works in your favor is that generally, creditors want to maintain a good relationship with their customers. Remember, a credit card company's favorite customer isn't the one who pays off their debt every month; it's the person who uses their card regularly, maintains a balance, and makes their payments regularly. If that sounds like you, then you have more leverage than you think. Even if you don't, creditors are more likely to respond to a customer who contacts them and asks them to do something, than customers who don't contact them at all.

Asking a Creditor to Remove a Late Payment Code

Getting a creditor to remove late payment codes from a credit report can often be pretty easy.

You can simply request a "goodwill adjustment" from the creditor. To do this, write a letter to the creditor explaining the situation that led to the late payment and asking the creditor to forgive it. This works much better with creditors you've had a good history with and many will be quite willing to help you out so long as you don't have a lot of late payments in your history.

Remember, you're talking to a fellow human being. Depending on how comfortable you are with voice communication (versus a typed conversation with an online representative) you may be better off initiating this conversation via phone. Either write out a brief script, or jot down some talking points to help you make an argument that your late payment was understandable. If you're not comfortable talking to another human being (more common than you might think), then use your talking points as part of your typed conversation with the online rep. Also, never get upset with a customer service rep, yell at them, or use foul language. You can't browbeat a customer service rep into submission. You can sweet-talk them. Don't be afraid to ask for a supervisor if you think you have a valid argument. Just ask nicely and stay polite. Some talking point ideas:

- Job loss: layoffs are pretty common these days. If you were late making a payment because you lost your job or switched jobs, you can certainly hope for a sympathetic response

- Health concerns: things like cancer, auto accidents, heart attacks, and other medical issues are often causes for late payments. Many customer service reps will be sympathetic if one of these issues was the cause of a late payment.

- Family emergency: maybe you've been tied up with a parent or child's health issues. Most people would be sympathetic to someone with this challenge and understand why you might have had to make a late payment.

- "I forgot:" it happens. Customer service representatives know it happens. You were working extra hours on a rush project, your kid was sick, you ended a relationship If you're going to use this one, follow it up by asking if they have a reminder email service that can help you avoid this mistake in the future. This works better if the late payment just happened, but if it wasn't too far back, you have a chance. As an added bonus, a sympathetic rep may also agree to waive the late penalty.

Automatic Payments Offer

Another useful approach is to offer to set up an automatic payments routine for your account. It shouldn't be surprising that businesses like the idea of money automatically being sent from a customer's bank account straight to their payments department. By the way, while you're using this tactic, see about asking for an interest rate reduction as a bonus.

If you go with an automatic payments option, don't think it means you can forget about your account. Check every time you charge something to the card to make sure your automatic payment is enough to at least meet the minimum payment requirement (your credit card company won't always tell you). By the way, if you are paying the minimum or close to it, try to increase your payment.

Disputing an Item

As you review your report, make note of any mistakes you find, big or small. Inform the creditor that you either want every error corrected or the entry pulled. Also, look for records or items that are more than seven years old, name misspellings, incorrect addresses, or accounts you closed that are being listed as closed by the creditor. Sometimes a creditor will pull the entry on an old account rather than going to the trouble to correct it.

Keep in mind too, there are two organizations involved, the creditor and the credit reporting company. If you strike out with one, you can still try disputing the issue with the other. Also, you have to dispute the item with every credit reporting company that has it on your credit report (there are exceptions to this). It's just not a good idea to fix it once and expect the credit report companies to follow on their own.

Mistakes happen more often than you might think. Sometimes your name gets recorded the wrong way (middle initials often get written down incorrectly), dates are misreported, or addresses are lost or changed.

Getting a Bankruptcy Dismissed

Bankruptcy does the most damage to your credit rating, so it's really tempting to try and get one removed from your credit report if you have one. Unfortunately it's not really possible, since bankruptcy proceedings are a matter of public record. If you can prove some errors in your bankruptcy documents that may help you get the bankruptcy dismissed, but you're still going to have the delinquencies that led to your bankruptcy on your credit report. Some credit repair companies make it sound like they can do it for you easily. Just pay their fee upfront they'll tell you.

Hiring a Credit Repair Company

There are companies that represent themselves as credit repair specialists as well as law firms that specialize in credit repair. While many of them are responsible, honest entities, some aren't. A reputable credit repair company won't promise a certain result. If you do decide to hire such a firm you shouldn't have to pay them up front. Generally, you'll save money and get the job done taking care of things by yourself and using a credit repair firm is not recommended. Still, if your time is particularly valuable, or your situation complicated, it might be worth it.

Negotiating

If you have a default on a credit card account, contact your creditor and ask them to remove it from your record (or mark it "Paid as agreed.") in return for your paying off the debt. Make sure they provide a written statement saying they agree to do this when you pay off the balance.

Chapter 5:
Keep Boosting Your Credit

The first thing you should do from this moment on, is if you have to make a late payment, call the creditor before you're late and explain the situation to their representative. Chances are they will offer you some extra time to make the payment or ask you just to pay the interest on your debt. Preventing late payment codes on your credit report is a solid pre-emptive strategy. Often, a creditor will be willing to give you a different payment date that better fits into your income stream. Make it a habit to check your credit card accounts twice a month at least if you access them online. More than a few credit card issuers have shortened the length of time a balance can go before you're charged interest.

Next, as a rule of thumb, try to keep your credit usage to no more than 30% of your available credit (20% would be even better, but you need to get below 10% to fully maximize your credit score). Each of your credit cards should be below this threshold. If you're in good shape overall, and expect it to be approved, asking for a credit limit increase on a card that's above this threshold should be okay. If it's a close call on the other hand, don't. Your risk of being refused and having this affect your credit score isn't worth it.

Don't close paid off credit card accounts! This reduces your overall debit to credit ratio, which hurts your credit score, and removes this card from your credit report at a certain point, which also hurts your credit score. Go ahead and use it from time to time (once or twice a quarter) to keep it active, but feel free to pay off the balance before interest is charged. It may be helpful to make multiple payments per month on a credit card to keep the balance at zero, provided your credit card company allows it.

It's better to have a couple of cards carrying balances and the rest with zero debt, so long as you're not surpassing that 30% threshold on either of the balance carrying cards.

Once you've achieved these goals, perhaps it's worth considering applying for an additional card and more credit, with the idea of improving your debt to credit ratio. While this can help your credit score, you have to balance it with the ways such a move hurts your score. It will result in an inquiry (not a big drop) and will also shorten your average account history time (another potential drop). If you have a good average account time, it's probably worth doing. If you don't, then you should look for other ways to help your credit score.

Loan Searches

As you read earlier, some loan searches can generate multiple inquiries that will be counted as one inquiry by credit reporting firms. If you're planning on getting a mortgage or auto loan, try to complete your loan search in a short amount of time. Less than 15 days is ideal, but less than 30 days should be okay.

Mix Things Up

This won't boost your score a lot, but if you're trying to raise it every possible point, it can help. One of the FICO categories is your credit mix. If you rely mainly on credit cards, then taking out a personal loan or buying something on installment payments will help. For most of us, car payments and mortgage or rent payments are our most common installment payments, but buying a new computer or stereo can also be done on payments. If you're focusing on improving your credit score, buying something via installments will help more than paying cash for the same item. If you take out the personal loan, think about using it to pay down any credit card debt you have to strengthen your debt to credit ratio. Don't do any of these things though unless you can be sure you'll pay them off on schedule.

Recovering From Bankruptcy

If you're reading this e-book because you're trying to rebuild your credit score after a bankruptcy, there is hope for you. The good news is that you can boost your credit score fairly easily and fairly quickly through a few simple steps. Unfortunately, regaining the lofty credit score you might have once had will be a good deal harder.

Since you should be in a better place from a debt standpoint, your low debt will help. Now you need to show you can handle credit again. Believe it or not you'll still be getting credit cards telling you you're "pre-approved," but that's not necessarily true. Some of those card offers will be rejected as soon as they discover your bankruptcy, while others will turn out to be "secured" credit cards, where you provide a security deposit in the amount you want your card's limit to be. This isn't a bad idea actually. Even a $200 credit limit gives you a starting point. Once you start charging things and making payments your credit score will start going up. Calculate your debit to credit utilization on the card by dividing the balance by the card's credit limit and multiplying by 100. One expert claims that the average debt utilization score average for those with a 760 credit score or higher is only 7%, so aim low for this one.

Chapter 6:
Common Mistakes

In this chapter you'll learn about common mistakes people make that can lower their credit scores. Some are easy to avoid; others are harder. Still, if you're trying to improve your credit score, it's important you stop doing the things that caused your score to decline.

Choose Your Cards Wisely

Try to stay away from store and gas cards. They tend to have higher interest rates and are easy to forget about. Every time you apply for one, you generate another credit inquiry. It can be tempting to sign up for a store card in order to get the discount that goes with it, but it generates a hard inquiry and another card to keep track of. These cards may not offer the same tools as big name credit cards (such as automatic payments or payment reminders). They're also not much use unless you're shopping in that store or gas station.

Should You Co-sign a Loan?

In a word, "No." You're putting your credit rating in the hands of someone else. Don't do it unless you can monitor the person closely enough to know that they're making their payments on time, and, you can afford to take over those payments if the other individual can no longer make the payments.

Don't Give In to Temptation

If you have good credit or better, you will receive a steady stream of new credit card offers. While it may be tempting to take advantage of these offers (it does improve your debt to credit ratio), each new card lowers your average account age, hurting your credit score.

Forgetting to Check Your Credit Reports

You can get one free copy of your credit report from each of the three nationwide credit reporting companies every 12 months. While you may have gotten all three in your initial effort to improve your score, in the future you might want to stagger your requests. If you plan on request one every four months, you can monitor your credit more carefully over the full year.

Letting Things Get Out of Control

It's not unusual for people to let their credit debt pile up. But as their credit card balances grow higher and higher and money becomes tighter and tighter, their credit issues become worse. Credit card companies monitor your credit rating and can raise your interest rate or lower your debt ceiling if they are so inclined. If you find yourself headed in this direction, take action! If you need to, meet with a non-profit credit counseling service, consider a debt consolidation loan, or borrow money from a relative to get things back under control.

Making Late Payments

You should avoid paying your credit card bills and loan payments late. Late payments automatically damage your credit score and as they pile up your credit rating declines. Most creditors will work with you if you contact them early. They can offer more time, or give you the option of paying just interest. FICO says a late payment can drop your credit score from 60 to 110 points depending on your score.

Closing Accounts

As you've already read, closing paid off accounts is a bad idea, especially if it's an account you've had a long time. Closing an account can hit you with a double whammy. First off, it damages your debt to credit ratio and second, it can decrease the average credit account age of your accounts. Keep the account and use it about once a quarter so the account holder doesn't close the account for inactivity.

Being Careless With Your Credit Cards

Credit card and identity theft are worrisome problems for consumers. While the credit card companies make an effort to spot dubious charges and alert you to them, you should be vigilant too! This includes pre-emptive efforts on your part. We were going to rent a car via a car deal once, until we noticed they had their customer's full credit card numbers posted on a white board behind the car rental desk. Another time, I was reciting my credit card number over the phone to pay for a food delivery, when I heard the person on the other end (in a crowded restaurant) repeating my card numbers out loud. I quickly asked her to stop doing that, before a bunch of diners obtained my information. Of course your risks are hardly limited to analog issues either. Card numbers are stolen during transactions all the time. If your credit card offers one use card numbers for online purchases, you should consider using them.

Also be sure to check your account or credit card statement at least monthly to check for charges that seem iffy. Your credit card company might be great about taking phony charges off your card, but they have to know a charge is iffy first. Don't skip by small charges you can't remember. Some credit card thievery goes on via a lot of small charges spread amongst a lot of different people's credit cards on the theory that such small charges are too much trouble to report.

Avoiding Credit Cards Entirely

It's no good to try to avoid having any credit cards either. This will actually hurt your credit score, since your credit and payment history is so important. As you read earlier, a creditor's favorite customer isn't the person who pays off their debt completely each month. It's the customer who has a balance on their account and makes payments regularly and on time.

Choosing the Wrong Credit Card

Credit cards come in all sorts of "flavors" these days. You can find low interest rate cards, cards that offer frequent flier miles, cards gear towards your particular interests, etc. You can also choose between gold, platinum, black, and blue cards, each with its own level of distinction. Spend some time deciding on what type of card is right for you. There's no sense paying an annual fee for an airline miles card if you don't plan on flying any time soon. Even worse would be applying for a card and getting turned down for it. You've gotten a hard inquiry and a credit denial at the same time.

Taking Cash Advances

While taking a cash advance won't automatically damage your credit score, cash advances suffer higher interest rates, and those rates begin at the time of the advance, not at the end of the normal grace period.

Getting Too Many Credit Cards

While having a lot of credit cards won't necessarily hurt your credit worthiness, it can hurt your wallet if many of them are annual fee cards. When applying for a card you should consider its costs (annual fees, APR) versus its benefits (miles, cash back, discounts).

Not Reading the Fine Print

Sure, credit card contracts are long, complex, and printed in small type, and carry all the emotional excitement of a stale cracker, but there are things in there that can cost you money or hurt your credit. Buried in that fine print is often language that tells you your interest rate will skyrocket if you miss a payment or get too close to your credit limit. It may also tell you that your 0% interest rate can be rescinded for the same reasons.

Maxing Out a Credit Card

FICO says maxing out a credit card can drop your credit score from 10 to 45 points depending on your credit score. A score of

680 will lose from 10 to 30 points. A score of 780 will lose from 25 to 40 points.

Tax Liens

If you suffer a tax lien, your credit score takes a hit. What's worse is tax liens stay on your report a long time. If paid, the lien stays on your report for seven years. If it's unpaid, it stays on your credit report for 10 years.

Conclusion

Thank you again for purchasing this book!

I hope this book was able to help you to improve your credit rating. While not the easiest of pursuits, your reward will be cheaper loans, credit cards, and a healthier financial outlook. Don't look at it as a one time goal. Maintaining a strong credit rating is a never ending task.

The next step is to continue managing your credit properly and avoid making any of the mistakes you read about in the last chapter. Here's an easy reminder list:

Avoid credit inquiries: each one made by a lender costs you five points off your credit score. Apply for new credit only after careful thought

No late payments: never miss a payment date. If you can't make the minimum payment, contact the lender and ask for their help. They may give you more time, or agree to let you pay just the interest.

Watch your debt to credit ratio: your goal should be to keep it under 10% to get the maximum benefit for your credit score. If you can't, at least try to keep it below 30%.

Use your leverage: lenders don't want to lose good customers. If you have a history of borrowing and paying, they will work to keep you. If you have a problem, offer to use an automatic payments option in return for their help. Another useful option is to take that offer for a new balance transfer card and play it against your current credit card company. While they may not offer a zero percent interest rate like the new card offer, you can probably get your interest rate reduced. Or, if it makes sense to take advantage of the new card offer and your current lender doesn't make a good enough response, go for it. Just remember, even though you're "pre-approved," it doesn't guarantee you'll get the new card, and it does mean you'll have another credit inquiry on your credit report.

Finally, if you enjoyed this book, please take the time to share your thoughts and post a review on Amazon. It'd be greatly appreciated!

Thank you and good luck!

www.ingramcontent.com/pod-product-compliance
Lightning Source LLC
Chambersburg PA
CBHW070414190526
45169CB00003B/1259